the GARFIELD book of CAT NAMES

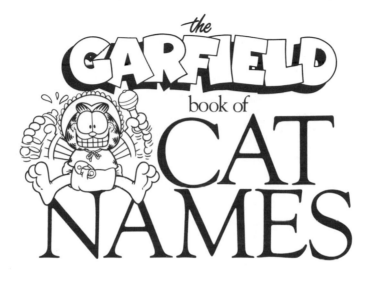

the GARFIELD book of CAT NAMES

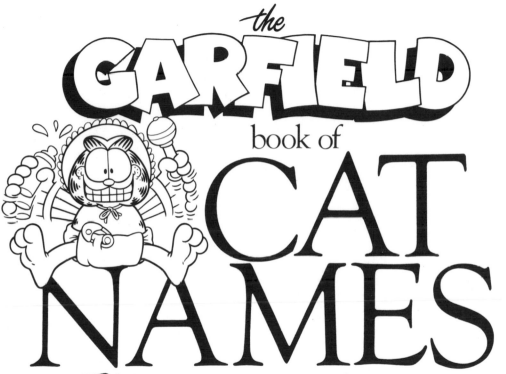

BY: JIM DAVIS *and* Carol McD. Wallace

Ballantine Books • New York

Library of Congress Catalog Card Number: 87-91355

ISBN: 0-345-35082-0

Manufactured in the United States of America
First Edition: August 1988
10 9 8 7 6 5 4 3 2 1

Contents

Foreword

Some cats go through life as "Kitty." Some owners don't see anything wrong with this. Robbing a feline of its individuality, denying it a proper, well-chosen name of its own; hey, it's all in a day's work. Nuts. Naming a cat is part of an owner's responsibility, like providing lasagna, a blanket, and a lifetime supply of kitty litter. A name a cat can wear with pride is just as important as the physical necessities. (Possibly not as important as the lasagna.)

Here are some other reasons to give your cat a name:

• So the vet can prescribe vitamins if it's puny.

• So you can call it and it won't come.

• So you can scream at it when it's shredded your drapes.

(These reasons are even more important if you're fortunate enough to have more than one cat.)

Picking the Right Name

The wrong name can spell disaster. What cat named "Twinkle" ever got picked first for touch football? Was any president of the Rotary Club ever named "Muffin"? Exactly. An appropriate name should allow plenty of room for growth, like an extra-large sweat suit. My own name recalls one of our country's finest presidents and has never given me a moment's embarrassment.

Directions for Naming Your Cat

1. Remember that it won't be a ridiculous kitten forever.
2. Make sure you know what sex it is. Consider John Wayne's embarrassment at being called "Marion" until they discovered he was "John."

3. Try calling the name out loud. Wouldn't you feel ridiculous screaming "Tulip!" at the top of your lungs?
4. Don't listen to anybody else's advice except mine. They aren't cats.

Using This Book

People must have a lot more time than cats (I've noticed this with Jon; he doesn't have the rigorous napping obligations I have), so maybe they can go through long alphabetical lists of names. My lists are shorter and they are divided by theme. If you already know that you want to name your cat after a food (a sound choice) then you can turn directly to that section. Some of the names have a history you might want to know about—like "Attila the Hun." Some names mean things. "Hugh," for example, means "intelligence," an attribute of all felines. I have put in histories and meanings. They may be perfectly accurate...and then again, they may not be.

Attribute Names

Sometimes people name their cats after a certain characteristic. Say it has white feet with lots of extra toes; you can call it "Bigfoot." If you got saddled with a Persian you might call it "Puff" for its long hair, but don't expect me to be its friend.

On the other hand, people sometimes breed cats for perverse purposes. There is a new breed of cats that have no hair. The kindly owner will tactfully rise above this characteristic and look for a name in another section of this book.

JAWS: Affectionate tribute to the carnivorous nature of felines. Not recommended for lady cats, no matter how large their appetites.

MITTENS: Unimaginative name inevitably given to cats with white paws. Lapses in personal hygiene result in gray paws. VAR: see "Snowshoe."

ROTUNDA: Latin for "round." Appropriate for plump female cat, but not very nice.

SNOWSHOE: Name for cats with extra toes on his white paws. Same cautions apply as for "Mittens."

WALLEYE: Well, there you are; not polite, but to the point.

SPEEDY: We cats, though often phlegmatic, are capable of quite a turn of speed. For instance, I've been clocked at 0 to 80 in 5 seconds when a hamburger was at stake.

BLACKIE: You can do better than that, Bud.

ALBINIA: Latin for "white." Warning: white cats are expert shedders, especially on dark clothes just back from the cleaners.

STRETCH: Refers to elasticity. Good name for very limber cat—unless he objects to being named after a rubber chicken.

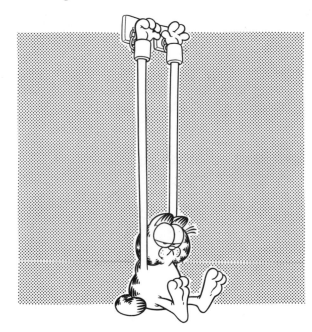

FLUFFY: Refers to unmanageable coat. Cream rinse would take care of this unfortunate condition.

WINK: Cats don't, so forget about it.

REX: Latin for "king." Good name for bossy type. Also, the name of disadvantaged breed of cat that looks like a cross between an undernourished Siamese and a sheep.

SMOKE: What a gray cat looks like when he hears a can opener in a distant room.

Names to Avoid

Some names get disqualified by association. You can't name your cat after the fat boy in third-grade homeroom, for instance. Or for the first woman to stand you up for a date, or for an axe-murderer. It's also important to respect the innate grace, wisdom, and dignity of felines. No cat ever comes when he's called, but believe me, he'll take to the streets if you name him something like "Lambykins."

BRUTUS: Fancy name for "brute," e.g. any dog smarter than Odie and bigger than me.

MARTY: Short for "Martin." Wears leisure suits and a diamond pinky ring and a toupee. A cat with no class at all.

POINDEXTER: Skinny guy with a loud plaid sportscoat, horn-rim glasses, and a big Adam's apple, three afflictions unknown among cats.

STRAD: Short for Stradivarius, the famous violin. Do you know what violins used to be strung with?

IRMA: The only person I've ever known who could put me off my food.

ZERO: Means "nothing" or "empty." As in, "this cat has zero personality" or "Jon has zero luck with women."

LYLE: If it were a human, it would be an accountant. What options does that leave for a feline?

TEMPERANCE: One of the seven cardinal virtues—used as a first name by the Puritans. I have no idea what it means.

SQUEAK: Please; it's a mouse name.

BELL: Device placed on cats by optimistic owners, to trace their whereabouts. SYN: Indignity.

Spiritual Names

Cats have always had an air of the otherworldly—in fact the ancient Egyptians had the good taste to worship us for around 2,000 years. Talk about "good old days"! Names dealing with the spiritual realm are very appropriate. And if you've been very good to your cat, it might put in a good word for you with the Big Guy Upstairs.

ADAM: The first man; the first litter-box changer.

VISNHU: Hindu supreme spirit, with four arms (also two legs). I could accomplish a *lot* with two extra arms.

GABRIEL: Angel who brings news. Appropriate for the one cat in a million who will carry a newspaper in its mouth.

BASTET: Egyptian cat goddess, whose specialty was fertility. Worship included annual orgies of food and drink and . . . food and drink.

BUDDHA: Large guy with protruding belly and calm disposition. Big on staring into space. Venerated by millions in the East. I want his job when he retires.

JEROME: Saint who translated the Bible into Latin and kept a cat that scholars say he fed a lot of lasagna to.

SAMSON: Strong man in the Bible, until he got a haircut. Good name for a Maine coon cat.

MOSES: Baby found in a basket. Good name for foundling cat, except the basket always holds three or more kittens.

NOAH: Lifeguard to the animal kingdom. Showed very poor judgment issuing boarding passes to dogs, spiders, and mail men.

ATHENA: Greek goddess of war, who sprang fully armed from her father Zeus' head. Forerunner of the migraine.

YVES: Patron saint of lawyers, often represented by a cat, which is like a lawyer in terms of intelligence, stealth, strategic abilities, discretion, and standing in the community.

SALOME: First recorded "exotic dancer"; the Rockettes owe everything to her.

THANKSGIVING: Act of giving thanks for the good things in life. Also, Garfield's favorite holiday—and believe me, not because of football.

Garfield's Old Buddies

Male bonding. Every fella needs some buddies to let down his fur with. No disrespect meant to the ladies, of course. But there are times in a cat's life when only the guy's guy will do. These are names for bachelors hanging out together; we all need moments like that.

JIM BOB: A good ol' boy who drives a pickup truck with a rifle rack and wears a cap to bed.

ED: Cat raised in a tree by squirrels. I couldn't persuade him to stay on the ground: he had a fear of low places.

SPEEDO: Neighborhood tough who rode a skateboard. He met an untimely end in a supermarket loading dock, buried under a pyramid of canned creamed corn.

SUSHI: Jon's goldfish. The only reason he's an old buddy is that Jon wouldn't let me turn him into a meal.

GUS: Short for "Augustus," a real handicap in life. Can be overcome by a scrappy kind of cat with a quick left.

BUCKET: My best friend in kittenhood. He lived in a galvanized tin pan in a corner of a movie theater and thrived on popcorn and Milk Duds. I hear he has heart trouble now.

HOWIE: Camp counselor who taught me all I know about the great outdoors; how to get back inside again!

GUIDO: Italian form of "Guy" or "guide." Tough guy I met in my brief but colorful stay behind bars.

Cat Names for People

It's considered an honor to name a baby after a relative or friend. So why not name a baby for a cherished cat? Here are some traditional cat names for parents without beloved cats of their own. If you already have a cat, then just use its name. The baby is sure to be the only "Felix" in its kindergarten class.

KIT: As in Kit Carson, the famous frontier scout. Expandable to Christopher, which might go over better with teachers and Boy Scout troop leaders.

KITTY: Pet name, expandable to Katherine or Kathleen if the baby deserves it.

CAT: Even a completely unimaginative cat owner with a taste for the obvious can find something better for his pet. For a human, though, it has a certain raffish charm.

GARFIELD: Name of one of the world's most illustrious cats, a handsome tiger of compelling intelligence, with a legendary way with females and sizzling stage presence. Any human should be honored by this name. It's good enough for a president of the United States.

Diminutives

"Diminutive," as those of us who write cat name books know, means a short version of a name. It also means "little," so some of these names refer to size. Not all cats are lucky enough to grow as big as me. It seems cruel to stress nature's inequities, but if you insist, here's how.

KEWPIE: Name of ridiculously cute doll. Appropriate for female equivalent of Nermal.

TEDDY: Short for "Theodore," or "gift of God." Also short for "teddy bear," a cat's best friend.

BABY: Why would you want to name a cat after one of its natural predators?

LITTLE JOHN: Ironic nickname for Robin Hood's enormous friend. Cats don't appreciate irony: they think it's humans showing off.

ODIE: Short on brains...as in "not playing with a full deck." Don't name a cat this unless it's beyond help or you hate it.

PATTY: Short for "Patricia." Also short for "mint patty," "hamburger patty," and "patty-cake." VARIANTS: Pattie, Pati, Patti.

MINETTE: French for "kitty." If you aren't French, this belongs to the "pretentious" category.

TINY: You'll be embarrassed as heck if your teeny little kitten grows to a robust size.

PEE WEE: You wanna give your pet a complex? Remember, cat shrinks are very expensive; the little couches are hard to come by.

MIGNON: French for "cute." Most often used to described a steak, as in, "I would like a cute steak for dinner."

PINKY: Short for "pinkeye," perhaps?

POOKY: A confidant: someone with whom to share secrets. Not to be confused with "Porky" which is found in another animal naming book.

Garfield's Mortal Enemies

A cat doesn't get to my position in life without stepping on a few feet here and there. Sure, I try to be sensitive to the little guys but, hey, you gotta do what you gotta do. I've been picked on too on the way up. So I'll admit it—I'm not a saint. I bear a grudge.

LIZ: My vet. Jon's crush. She doesn't do either of us any favors.

MR. POSTMAN: In the natural order of things, mailmen are cats' traditional prey. It's just too bad so few cats know this. And so few postmen.

BOBO: A tough guy. Not a cat to meet in a dark alley.

JEAN: First name of the founder of Weight Watchers. I'd like to make a dart board out of her.

NERMAL: World's cutest kitten. BLECCH!

FIFI: A French poodle—a freak of nature handicapped by a lousy haircut. I always make an effort to restore Fifi to nature's design, but Fifi never appreciates this.

LIBRA: Latin for "scale." Get it?

SPOT: Spot is a dog's name; enough said.

Food Names

Basically, people name babies and pets after what's important to them; beloved relatives, figures in history they admire, or maybe saints. What's important to me is food, and if more people were honest with themselves they'd admit that it was important to them, too. You realize this when you see how many names you think are about something else actually refer to—guess what?—eating.

For my other big interest see the section on sleep.

JAMOCA: Hey, man, hipster jive talk for the elixir of life: *coffee.*

MILKSHAKE: Combination of ice cream and milk popularly consumed as dessert, breakfast, or cocktail. Good name for a fluffy beige cat—or a pink one for that matter.

HOMINY: Southern corn dish of American Indian origin. DIM: Grits.

COCOA: Warm drink made with milk and chocolate. Not to be confused with homonym "Coco," first name of famous and skinny fashion designer.

MOUSSE: Could be one of three things: fancy name for pudding; large, not very bright antlered animal; or hair gunk, stuff no self-respecting cat would touch.

CARBO: Short for "carbohydrate," the stuff that makes life worth living.

HOT DOG: Frankfurter. Also, derisive epithet for a show-off. As in, "Listen, hot dog, have you been climbing the drapes again?"

KIEV: Russian city where butter squirts out of all the food.

MACARONI: Yankee Doodle came to town
A-riding on a pony,
Put a feather in his hat
And called it "macaroni."
What I want to know is, Why?

NACHO: The Mexican answer to lasagna; Olé!

Foreign Names

I don't really see the use of traveling. If God had wanted us to go on trips, we would have built in odometers. Travel is supposed to broaden your mind—but my mind is the only narrow thing about me and I like it that way.

Travel is very fashionable though, and the farther you go, the better. (Going to the farm to see Jon's parents doesn't make it at all.) Then you have to prove you've been there, with dopey souvenirs and boring snapshots, and keep reminding people. That's why you give a cat a foreign name.

HEIDI: Kitten from Switzerland who wears her ears in braids.

JACQUES: French for "James," not "Jack." (You can tell I've done my research.) But why not just call the cat "Jack" instead of having to correct everyone all the time?

SOLANGE: French girl's name, means "good shepherdess." Cats don't get along with sheep.

CASIMIR: Greeting from the mysterious East, home of turbans and pointy-toed slippers.

MARIO: "Warlike," in Italian. Between the naps and making all that lasagna I wonder when they have time to fight.

GASTON: If you can live with a cat that eats snails and smokes strong cigarettes, be my guest.

SOPHIA: Means "wisdom." Sophia Loren's name. She's Italian. She probably makes great lasagna. Probably loves cats. Loves making lasagna for cats. Where's my passport?

CARMEN: As in Carmen Miranda, famous Brazilian singer/dancer with hats made of unprocessed fruit salad.

ASTRID: Teutonic for "impulsive in love." Swedish beauty with long blond hair who doesn't have the time of day for a mere cat.

HANS: One of the ninety-seven forms of "John." DIM: Hansel. Everyone will ask where Gretel is.

SOMBRERO: What you take a siesta under.

LUBATUWO: Famous thirteenth century warrior king of small African country now part of Burkini Faso. (I made that up.)

Geographic Names

Geography is about important places, like history is about important people. Places are important because important things happen there, like battles and the invention of different foods. Sometimes they are named after famous people, like Bismarck, North Dakota. This selection lists some of the significant spots on the globe, but you could think of your own. Like where you got your first speeding ticket. The town you went to college in. Where your grandparents came from. Where your favorite chocolate bar is made. Go on—name your cat "Hershey."

MANHATTAN: A kind of clam chowder, inferior to "New England."

VEGAS: American center for flashy personalities and Mecca for showbiz types like myself. I can see it now, in six-foot-high neon lights on the strip, "Garfield Sings!"

BREADBASKET: U.S. region where wheat is produced, as in "breadbasket of the nation." Also, human anatomy, as in "you look out or I'll hit you in the breadbasket." Also, literally, basket for bread.

BOLOGNA: Pronounced "baloney." Italian town responsible for the invention of luncheon meat.

EVEREST: The highest mountain in the world, the ultimate challenge to mountain climbers. Maybe a name for the ultimate challenge to live with. I'm not talking about me, I'm talking about *Odie*.

STRASBOURG: Town in France where geese are force-fed, a concept I don't understand.

MISSISSIPPI: River that has deep, dark mud named after a kind of chocolate pie.

EGYPT: Middle Eastern country where cats used to be worshipped.

Old Girlfriends

Of course a devastatingly attractive cat like me has quite a history with the females of the species. (Thankfully I've never had to undergo the humiliation Jon suffers; but then, look at Jon.) I wouldn't want to brag, but sometimes I wish I weren't *quite* so alluring to them. After all, I'll always be faithful to the love of my life—ME.

AMY: French for "beloved." We had a great time until she wanted me to leave my blanket at the house. I just wasn't ready for a commitment.

BIJOU: She was a gem, all right, if you like the high heels and lots of jewelry type. Personally, I think they look stupid on a cat.

CRISPINA: Latin, feminine form of Cri-

spin, meaning "curly-haired." Sounds like a breakfast cereal to me.

PRISCILLA: Latin for "of ancient lineage." There was nothing prissy about the one I knew; she drank out of Odie's water bowl on our first and last date.

ARLENE: Arlene's basic appeal—she's got *great taste*.

BABE: Name to use in preliminary stages of relationship. As in, "Hey, babe, what's happening?", "Hey, babe, wanna have dinner with me?", or "Oh, babe, you have the most beautiful whiskers."

TAMMY: VARIANTS: Tammie, Tami, Tamee (tackee). Nice chassis, nothing under the hood. Perfect for the drum majorette kind of cat.

MARGOT: Diminutive for "Margaret." She liked caviar. A class act; almost too classy for me.

FATIMA: The only Siamese I've ever dated. Blue eyes to die for, but a voice like claws on a blackboard.

ZOE: Greek for "life." I only took her out so I could say I'd dated cats from "A to Z."

33

Names from History

I was going to fill this section with cats I admired in history, but the big hitters of the feline world seem to have kept their exploits to themselves. This is typical of feline discretion. It forces me to turn to overachievers among humans, who aren't as modest. (You should hear Jon bragging about his golf games.)

It's a pretty bloodthirsty group, but that's what I admire; folks who know what they want and get it.

GENGHIS KHAN: "Perfect Warrior." He adopted the name once he decided what he wanted to be. It goes to show what you can accomplish when you set your mind to something.

NAPOLEON: Short Corsican general who conquered Europe and gave his name to a pastry.

34

JULIUS CAESAR: Roman general whose motto was, "I came, I saw, I conquered." I feel like that after every meal.

ATTILA THE HUN: Warrior king who invaded Europe, famous for the utter destruction he and his troops left behind.
DIM: "The Scourge of God."

VICTORIA: Queen of England, Empress of India, and quite a gal. Good name for a plump cat who stands on her dignity.

ANASTASIA: Supposed only survivor of Russian royal family; good name for a cat inclined to put on airs.

MARIE ANTOINETTE: French queen who had her head cut off for suggesting a change in the French national diet.

MERLIN: Famous magician. Brilliant at making things disappear. I can do that. . . .
He could also make things change shapes—I can do that, too.
I guess this means that the multi-talented Garfield is also a magician. Maybe that's how I'll get to Vegas!

NIMROD: "The mighty hunter." My spiritual brother; never mind that all I ever hunt is hamburgers.

JULIETTE: Name of founder of the Girl Scouts and inventor of the great feline sport, mugging Girl Scouts for their cookies.

LOUIS: Any one of seventeen kings of France, several of whom wore Dolly Parton hair and high heels.

35

ROBIN HOOD: I approve of hanging out in the forest to surprise people, but his technique needed refinement. It should have been: Take from the rich and give to *cats*.

DAVY CROCKETT: Frontiersman and hunter, famous for hunting bears and taming wildcats. (No relation to me.) Best of all, he gave the world the coonskin cap.

Literary Names

Since cats can't read, you might be wondering where I got these ideas. Culture, my friend, is in the air, free for all of us to breathe and absorb. Of course, cats have pretty small nostrils so absorption is selective. I usually stick to the Classics Illustrated Comics.

JULIET: Underage heroine of famous love story. Appropriate for cat who likes to moon around on balconies.

KITTY: Heroine of long, long, long book called *War and Peace*. Nobody will ever believe you read the whole thing. They'll also think you were just lazy and couldn't think up a better name for your cat. Then you will have wasted the price of this book.

MEDUSA: Unpleasant character with snakes for hair. One look at her turned people to stone. That could be a pretty useful technique.

POLLYANNA: Sappy heroine of children's story; perpetual optimist, in spite of all the evidence, including Monday mornings.

FALSTAFF: Fat friend of the hero in Shakespeare's plays about Henry IV. No one ever talked about putting him on a diet. I was born too late.

CAPTAIN AHAB: Monomaniacal fisherman. Good name for a cat with a one-track mind.

LINUS: A towering figure in contemporary fiction. The other thing we have in common is we appreciate the value of a good blanket.

KATZENJAMMER: German for "cats yowl." Appropriate for the highly verbal cat with musical aspirations.

MEHITABEL: Intellectual's version of pin-up cat. Her biography was written by a typing cockroach. Obviously she wasn't very choosy about her friends.

MORGAN: Witch in fairy tale who created castle made entirely of food. This is someone I'd like to meet.

WOLF: Short for "Big Bad Wolf," who scared the pajamas off Little Red Riding Hood. Nice name for a cat with big teeth.

PUSS IN BOOTS: DERIVATION: Song by Nancy Sinatra, "These Boots Are Made for Walking." Strong-minded female cat who won't stand for any nonsense.

Morons I Have Known

I considered putting Jon in this category, since as we all know he can be a real idiot, particularly where women are concerned. But I relented. After all, he's had the intelligence to stick with *me*.

It's not a big category but I know it won't be a very popular one, either. After all, how dumb can a cat be?

HANSEL & GRETEL: Anybody knows that a trail of breadcrumbs scattered in the forest is going to get eaten. In a forest even *I* would eat breadcrumbs.

HEYWOOD: Writer who started the rumor that all cats are gray in the dark.

CHRISTOPHER COLUMBUS: What if the world had been flat? He would have sailed right off the edge. How smart is that?

ALICE: Silly blonde who fell down a rabbit hole and kept eating and drinking mysterious substances. Doesn't everyone's mother tell them not to take food from a stranger?

Music Names

You may think of me as a fat, lazy slob who only cares about sleep and food. But beneath my imposing exterior lurks the soul of a musician. I am often moved to tears by songs like "O Sole Mio" (Oh, my filet of sole) and "Che gelida manina" (What jellied manna). Through all the many trials of my life I stick to the motto: "It ain't over 'til the fat cat sings."

FORTE: Loud enough to wake everyone in the house. VAR: Fortissimo, loud enough to wake everyone a block away.

PIZZICATO: Probably means "played as if in a drunken state." Couldn't apply to a cat (have you ever seen a drunken cat?), but sounds nice.

41

TUBA: Large brass instrument that makes noises like a giant digestive tract.

VIOLA: Stringed instrument whose case is just the right size for a cat nap.

LARGO: Tempo indication meaning "lethargic," though I prefer to think of it as "favoring economy of motion."

TRIANGLE: What the dummies in the marching band play.

ARIA: The good part of the opera, where the star gets to sing the tune.

ALTO: Low female voice. Agitated Siamese.

TENOR: High male voice; cats courting. That would be quite a high tenor.

BASS: Deep. As in the purring of a very large, very happy elderly tomcat.

SOPRANO: Highest voice—hungry kitten or very angry cat.

CARUSO: Legendary tenor. I could give him a run for his money if I could only get a better agent.

Nature Names

Jon is the real nature lover. I don't like to swim unless I can see the turquoise concrete. You can't take a TV on a camping trip because trees don't have electrical outlets.

There are no sandboxes, screen doors, or refrigerators for the comfort and amusement of pets. You can't order out for pizza.

And then, life in the wild can be dangerous. The leaves in the salad crisper don't give you diseases—but look at poison ivy. Normal house insects don't bite, they just compete with you for dinner—but look at red ants. Inside, mice are pests—outside, there are bears. Don't step out the door: IT'S A JUNGLE OUT THERE!

I always was a house cat.

TIGER: Common name for "Felis tigris," boldly-striped member of the feline family, not unlike myself in looks and temperament.

43

ROCKO: Also, "Rocco." Saint who cured Italians of the plague; also term for someone with minerals where the brains usually go.

BUNNY: Another revoltingly cute animal, not very bright and with sadly deformed ears. Don't name a cat after an animal so far below it on the phylogenetic scale.

CLOUDY: Weather condition in which my sunbeam is obscured. Also, what Odie's water bowl looks like when Jon forgets to change it for a week.

SKY: One of those hippie names like "Rainbow" or "Season," for vegetarians with macrame kitty beds and tie-dye blankeys.

RANGER: A cat's best friend in our national parks—he's the guy who knows where the exit is.

HERBIE: Short for "Herbert," meaning "glorious warrior." Jon had a pet frog named Herbie once. I had a pair of frogs legs named Herbie shortly afterward.

IVY: A clinging vine. Unlikely to suit a cat, unless she's very neurotic.

SASSAFRAS: "A small genus of aromatic North American...trees with soft yellow wood,...dioecious yellow flowers in umbellate racemes, a six-lobed perianth, and nine stamens in three rows." (Webster's 3d International Dictionary)

ICICLE: For the cold-hearted.

FERN: A tender, yielding green plant; also, a terrific between-meal snack.

DAISY: Diminutive of "Margaret," don't ask me why. A sweet, old-fashioned kind of name, and a plant with great recreational potential.

FAUNA: Also, Fawna, baby deer. Like "Bunny"; nice house, nobody home.

PEARL: White beads made by oysters. My birthstone is the only one that's also a food by-product.

People's Names for Cats

It's considered a compliment to name a baby for a family member or friend. Obviously, it's even more of a compliment to give a person's name to a cat, who is sure to do it justice.

You can name a cat after your best friend, or your sister, or your boss who's sure to be flattered. Or pick one of these names—including nicknames and their derivations—carefully selected for you by the world's expert on cat names, ME.

DOC: Jon's brother, also known as "Doc Boy." Believe it or not, Jon got all the looks in the family.

ROY: From French for "roi," or "king." A name that evokes mystery and power, as in "Evil Roy Gato" and "Roy Rogers."

RUBY: Red precious stone. Generally an older woman who calls you "hon."

VICTOR: Stuffy name for "the guy who won."

ANGELA: DIM: Angie. Good name for slightly daffy blonde kitten.

JAKE: Short for "Jamoca." See *Food Names.*

CHIP: Short for "chocolate chip."

CHUCK: Short for "ground chuck."

JOE: Short for "sloppy Joe."

JON: World's most common name. There are 93 different forms of it in 27 languages. I'm afraid my Jon is just as undistinguished as his name.

BETTY: Short for "apple brown betty," or "dessert with Garfield's name on it."

MARY: Most common female name. From Hebrew for "bitterness." VARIANTS: Maria, Marie, Maura, Marilyn, Mamie, Muriel, Marilla, Mariquita, etc., etc. Unimaginative for a person; kind of cool for a cat.

PHIL: Short for "fill Garfield up."

Presidential Names

There's no greater honor in the world than being President of the United States of America. And there's no greater honor for a cat than having a president's name. These aren't names for silly kittens like Nermal. These names have resonance. They're history. They're statesmanship. They're greatness.

COOLIDGE: President known for his taciturnity, a quality shared by most cats.

MADISON: Husband of Dolly Madison who first served ice cream in the White House.

TYLER: The president everybody forgets about when they're trying to list all the presidents. (He was tenth.)

HAYES: Was given first Siamese in America, and liked it. A seriously misguided man.

FORD: Cornerstone of the great American tradition of football-playing presidents.

POLK: Umm. Short for polka-dot?

TAFT: A man of majestic proportions, not unlike myself.

Pretentious Names

Some humans think of pets as an extension of their own personalities. It's true that dogs and their owners look alike but cats aren't that easily influenced. If you want a cat as decoration, it might cooperate. Or it might be like me. I know my own strengths, and decorative I'm not. On the other hand, I do make Jon a lot more interesting. How many people do you think would read a cartoon strip about *him*?

People who think of pets as accessories give them show-off names that prove how sophisticated they are, but you can't fool me.

COLETTE: French writer who was very fond of cats, but isn't that famous. Real graduate-student kind of name.

PICASSO: Ultra-famous Spanish painter. Not very convincing if you want to show off your culture since everybody in the world has heard of him.

MAX: Short for Maximilian, maybe? Maxwell? Maximum? Maximum snob appeal, if you ask me.

NUREYEV: Great Russian ballet dancer, famous for his leaps. Good name if you can't think of anything else, since every cat prides itself on its grace.

ODYSSEUS: Ancient Greek who got lost on his way home from a war. Admirable name for a tomcat with an adventurous nature.

HARLEQUIN: Fancy clown, dressed in black and white. Cats never clown without very good reason: like lasagna.

VITRUVIUS: Ancient Roman architect. Show-off name because nobody knows who he is except real know-it-alls like myself.

PRINCIPESSA: That's "princess" to the hoi polloi.

MAGNUM: If you have a TV show in mind, you're a real person. If you plan to name your pet after a big bottle of champagne, I'm not so sure.

BÉBÉ: French for "baby." If that's what you want to name a pet, buy a tiny dog.

Rock 'n' Rollers

Cats have a natural affinity for rock music. They like to chase their tails on the drum heads, boogey across the keyboard, sharpen their claws on guitar strings. On the whole, we go in for heavy metal (remember what those acoustic guitars are strung with), though I am also a great fan of Whitney Houston.

MICHAEL: Good name for the rare cat born wearing dark glasses and one white glove.

FABIAN: Male vocalist with bouffant hair-style. Name comes from Latin for "bean farmer." Seriously.

BEATLE: How to name one cat for the Fab Four. Good choice for a long-hair.

MEATLOAF: Call him "Mr. Loaf" until you know him better.

TINA: Diminutive of "Christine." Can you imagine how far "Ike and Christine" would have gotten?

STING: Grown man who used to prance around in yellow and black tights. Not a good role model for a cat.

CATS WAULER: The future name of yours truly when my career gets rolling and I'm playing the stadium dates.

ELVIS: Old Norse mean "all-wise," though that doesn't explain the sequin bell-bottoms.

WHAM!: The noise the screen door makes when Jon opens it suddenly and I'm hanging on the outside.

PETER, PAUL & MARY: The perfect group name for a small litter of kittens.

55

Cats have more sense than to run around working up a sweat in the name of fun. Besides, "Odie-Baiting" lacks poetry as a name.

For other recreational activities, see "Sleep."

Sidekicks

The Caped Avenger leads a swashbuckling existence, but his life was slightly empty until he met up with his trusty sidekick Slurp. Not only that—it was a lot more aggravating.

The sidekick's role is to be supportive, smooth the way for the hero, and ask dumb questions to make the hero feel smarter. Not unlike the owner–pet relationship. In fact, if you're really honest, you might want to think about who's the sidekick: you or your cat?

SANCHO PANZA: "Panza" is Spanish for "pot belly." He was the brains behind Don Quixote.

V.P.: Short for Vice President, the quintessential sidekick.

CUPID: The little guy who does all the dirty work for Venus, goddess of love.

WATSON: Victim of Sherlock Holmes' condescension. He couldn't be as dumb as he pretended if he wrote down all those stories.

ROBIN: The only one who really knows how to operate all the optional features on the Batmobile.

JIMMY OLSON: Dorky cub reporter in bow tie who gets in trouble so Superman can rescue him.

TONTO: Loyal Indian who hangs out with horseman in a Halloween mask.

Sleep Names

There are two ideas about sleep. Some people say, "You can sleep when you're dead" and boast about sleeping only four hours a night. The other attitude is, "It's a third of your life so you might as well enjoy it." You can guess which way I feel. Fortunately I'm not one of those types who need elaborate props to sleep. No, sir: no silk sheets, no earplugs, no hot toddies for this cat! I just respond to the call of nature...

SNOOZE: Affectionate nickname for the main activity. VAR: slumber, doze

NARCOLEPSY: Fancy word for nap attacks.

RIP: Short for Rip van Winkle, henpecked husband who went drinking with dwarves and passed out for 20 years. Suitable for cat who likes *long* naps.

MR. SANDMAN: The guy who sprinkles sand in your eyes to make you sleep. I personally have never had to resort to this technique.

SLEEPING BEAUTY: A pretty light sleeper if a kiss was enough to wake her up!

NOD: As in, "to nod off to sleep."

59

SIESTA: Naptime in foreign countries where it gets hot during the day and they eat dinner after my bedtime.

HIBERNATION: Sleeping all winter. Even I think this is taking things a little too far.

SLOTH: Lazy, slow-moving mammal that lives in South American trees. Also, what I feel like on Monday morning.

LULLABY: Song you sing to make a baby sleep. Nice idea, wasted on babies.

SOMNAMBULA: Fancy name for woman who walks in her sleep. I occasionally do this and miraculously find myself in front of the refrigerator. Then, for a real peak experience, I eat in my sleep.

Unisex Names

There's a fad now for unisex names. They're supposed to sound classy, but so many little kids have them that they just sound bratty. Plus, it's harder than ever to tell little girls and little boys apart.

Still, there may be people out there who don't have access to a vet, and can't tell what kind of cat they have. I offer these names as a service to spare the world more cats named "Thomasina" and "Bobette."

HILARY: From Latin meaning "cheerful." As in "hilarious." For the unusual cat who's easily amused.

ASHLEY: Wimpy character in *Gone With the Wind* who Scarlett O'Hara falls in love with even though Rhett Butler could eat him for breakfast.

COURTNEY: Leans toward the girlish; a fat little blonde with sausage curls. Save this for a last resort.

PAGE: Young man who used to serve a knight. I need a page to bring me breakfast in bed and to tie the Caped Avenger's cape. I wonder if Jon could be trained to do it?

BLAIR: "From the field" in Gaelic. Completely nondescript unless it's also your mother-in-law's name. Of course she'll be flattered to have a cat named for her, especially if you have children shortly afterward and name them for characters in your favorite soap opera.

Conclusion

Now you know which names are good for your cat, and which names will cause him to use your shoes as a litter box. If none of these names seems appropriate, better double-check the cat: you may actually be trying to name an armadillo or toaster by mistake. Of course, as a last resort, you could always name your cat "Anonymous," in which case your cat will surely think of a few choice names to call *you*! In the final analysis, however, it doesn't really matter what you name your cat, because cats don't care what you call them, just as long as you call them for dinner.